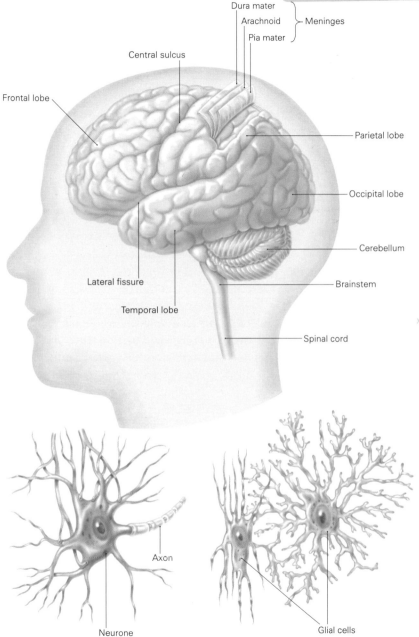

Figure 1: Side view of the brain showing the outer brain structure and nerve cells

How do fits happen?

To understand how a fit or seizure can happen, it is helpful to know something about the normal workings of the brain. The brain is made up of billions of cells known as neurones (see Figure 1).

Neurones connect to each other so that their electrical signals or discharges are co-ordinated and timed according to the need of the various activities of the body. The neurones use chemicals called neurotransmitters to transmit their electrical signals. These chemical transmitters are either *excitatory*, in which case they stimulate other neurones or they are *inhibitory*, in which case they suppress or stop messages to other neurones.

The effect of one neurone on another is a co-ordinated action. A seizure may occur if this co-ordination is disrupted. The amount and type of the disruption will have an effect on the type, length and severity of the seizure. Anyone can have a fit when the normal neurotransmitter co-ordination mechanism is disturbed. It is only when fits are unprovoked and keep occurring that the term epilepsy is used. The term epilepsy is different from seizure. You cannot have epilepsy without having seizures, but you can have a seizure without necessarily having epilepsy.

What causes epilepsy?

The causes of epilepsy are divided into three main groups.

1. Idiopathic (primary) epilepsy
In this group, no obvious cause for the epilepsy can be found but there is a possibility that for some types there may be a **genetic** link. About 60 per cent of affected people have idiopathic epilepsy.

2. Cryptogenic epilepsy
In this group the cause is suspected but cannot actually be confirmed by specific tests.

3. Symptomatic (secondary) epilepsy
In this group there is an identifiable cause. Examples of possible causes include head injury, **meningitis, encephalitis,** a brain tumour, or birth injury due to

lack of oxygen during or immediately after birth. Symptomatic epilepsy can happen at the time of the damage to the brain or at a later stage.

Can epilepsy be inherited?
Most forms of epilepsy appear not to be inherited, although for some of the less common types, such as juvenile myoclonic epilepsy, there may be a small increased risk that children of the affected person will develop epilepsy.

Are there different types of fit?

Not everyone with epilepsy has the same type of fit. There are two main groups and a number of different types within each group. The two main groups are *generalised seizures* and *partial seizures*. When the first abnormal electrical discharge arises from both sides of the brain this is known as a generalised seizure. When the first abnormal electrical discharge arises from one specific part of the cerebral hemisphere this is known as a partial seizure.

Generalised seizures
During generalised seizures, the abnormal electrical discharge arises from both sides of the brain at the same time and the signs are seen on both sides of the body. There are six types of generalised seizure.

1. Absences
These are fits that mainly affect children, where for between five and 20 seconds a child briefly loses awareness of his or her surroundings. Absences can happen several times a day and affect a child's performance at school. There may also be eye fluttering or lip-smacking movements during the absence attack.

2. Myoclonic jerks
These are short, shock-like contractions of different muscle groups anywhere in the body but usually in the arms and legs. The jerks last for a fraction of a second and the person can fling a limb and throw an object held in the hand involuntarily.

3. Atonic or astatic seizures
These cause an immediate relaxation of muscles so that the person may suddenly fall to the ground, sometimes injuring themselves as they fall.

4. Tonic seizures

These seizures last between five and ten seconds and lead to a sudden contraction of whole body muscles, which causes the person to fall, and sometimes to injure themselves as they fall.

5. Clonic seizures

During these seizures there are sudden, rhythmic contractions of groups of muscles causing jerking and twitches of various muscle groups which may last up to two minutes.

6. Tonic clonic seizures

These seizures have two stages: they start with a tonic phase with stiffness followed by a clonic phase with rhythmic contractions. The whole seizure may last between one and three minutes. If these seizures recur without the person regaining consciousness then the condition is very serious and is termed *status epilepticus*.

Partial seizures

In partial seizures, the abnormal electrical discharge starts in one part of the brain and may spread to another part of the brain. This spread is known as *secondary generalisation*. The person sometimes feels the symptoms of the abnormal electrical discharge in the part of the body controlled by the specific brain area that is being affected. If the person remains conscious during the fit then it is known as a *simple partial seizure*, but if the level of consciousness is affected then the term *complex partial seizure* is used.

People who have simple partial seizures often describe changes in **sensory perception** such as a strange taste or smell, sudden fearfulness or a feeling of familiarity with events, which had never previously been encountered ("deja vu"). These unexpected thoughts are a result of abnormal electrical discharge starting in the temporal lobe of the brain, which is the area of the brain responsible for processing various thoughts and emotions. If the electrical discharge starts in another area, the person may complain of tingling or numbness in one of their limbs or face depending on the neurones affected and the progression of the abnormal electrical spread.

Complex partial seizures

The seizures can either start as *simple* and progress or start as *complex* from the outset, with confusion and sometimes strange behaviour such as lip smacking, with no memory of the event. Simple and complex partial seizures can progress to generalised tonic clonic seizures (secondary generalisation).

There are some other older terms, which are still in common use. *Grand mal* means a generalised tonic clonic seizure wheather the onset is partial or generalised. *Petit mal* is another name for absences of the generalised type. *Temporal lobe seizures* mean simple or partial seizures arising from the temporal lobe of the brain.

The term *aura* is used to describe the warning that a seizure is about to happen. The aura is in fact the start of the abnormal electrical activity in the brain before a seizure spreads to other neighbouring areas of the brain.

Seizures do not seem to injure the brain unless they quickly recur without the person regaining consciousness and they last more than 30 minutes. Many people have dozens of seizures in their lives without intellectual or physical injury. Extremely rarely, a seizure can cause suffocation and death. This occurs in about one in 400-600 people with active epilepsy and is known as *Sudden unexpected death in epilepsy syndrome*. People with well-controlled epilepsy are less at risk than those experiencing daily, generalised seizures. This is a particularly important reason for people with epilepsy to take their drugs regularly. Failing to take the drugs regularly also increases the risk of accidents such as falls, drowning and non-stop seizures, a condition known as *status epilepticus*. This condition is a medical emergency that requires urgent hospital admission and intensive care.

Epilepsy syndromes

A syndrome is a group of symptoms and signs that occur together in a way that is non-coincidental. Epilepsy syndromes tend to start at a specific age and proceed in a reasonably set pattern. It is therefore possible in many cases to predict their outcome and their response to medication.

The syndromes can be *benign*, in which case they do not have harmful consequences. The best example of this is *Benign Rolandic epilepsy of childhood*. In this condition the seizures occur during sleep in older children. The electric discharge is from a specific area on the surface of the brain, known as the Rolandic fissure and the child will grow out of the seizures without the need for treatment in most cases.

Juvenile onset myoclonic epilepsy also starts in young people and causes specific types of seizure and **EEG** abnormalities. The seizures occur on awakening and are associated with body jerking and sensitivity to flickering light. This condition is usually straightforward to control, but requires life-long treatment.

A rare type of epilepsy is *Lennox-Gastaut syndrome*, which starts in childhood and may have an effect on intellectual development and may be hard to control. Children with Lennox-Gastaut syndrome may need special schooling or sometimes residential care. There are many causes for Lennox-Gastaut syndrome including meningitis and brain damage before or during the time of birth, or in the early stages of development.

Some young babies will start by having another rare and severe epilepsy syndrome called *West syndrome* in the first year of life and then go on to develop Lennox-Gastaut syndrome in the second or third year of life.

How is epilepsy diagnosed?

When a fit first happens the person, family or friends are naturally concerned and medical advice, usually from the GP is required immediately. If at all possible, the doctor will want to interview someone who can give a first hand account of the event. The diagnosis depends to a large extent on the description given by someone who has seen the fit or on other information given by the person who has had the fit.

All other tests are not really 'diagnostic' except when a fit is recorded while the person is having an EEG test (see below). Recording a fit during an EEG is very rare, as fits are unpredictable and infrequent in most people. Taking an accurate record of what happened is therefore the most crucial part of the diagnosis and on many occasions making the diagnosis has to be postponed until a reliable witness can be interviewed by a doctor.

Electroencephalography (EEG)
This test is used to record the minute electrical impulses produced by the activity of the brain. The test is carried out in special departments, which are only available in some hospitals. You may be referred to another larger hospital that can carry out the test. During the test, you will be asked to lie or sit in a comfortable chair. A special glue (which can be removed after the test) is used

1003181670т

to secure a disc conduction wire to the scalp (see Figure 2).

The machine only receives signals from the brain and does not itself send any electrical signals. The test is therefore completely harmless. After the wires are

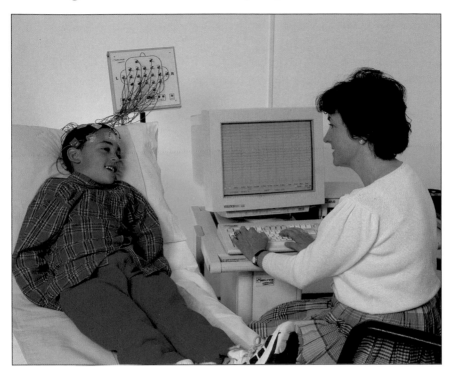

Figure 2: A child having an EEG test

connected you will be asked to close your eyes, breath deeply and a strobe light will be used to try to cause seizure activity in the brain. The test takes about 30-45 minutes to complete and sedative drugs are not normally used, except for young children or for people who are confused or find it very difficult to remain still during the test.

Over the years, EEG has developed and it is now possible to combine EEG recording with video so that constant monitoring can take place over several days in a special room. If a fit does occur, then its type and electrical discharge can be recorded at the same time. This combined recording is known as EEG-video telemetry. This is particularly useful when the diagnosis is uncertain and if brain surgery for epilepsy is being considered.

The EEG test is not conclusive, and sometimes people with true epilepsy have a normal EEG and those without epilepsy may show some abnormality. The EEG test only records a 20-30 minute period of daily brain activity and may therefore miss an abnormality that is short and sudden. The chance of an EEG showing clear epileptic abnormality in a person with epilepsy is about 50:50. When a diagnosis of epilepsy is strongly suspected, techniques may be used to deliberately cause a fit and the most widely used one is sleep deprivation, where the person is asked to stay awake the night before the test. Lack of sleep is one of the most important triggers of fits in people with epilepsy. As well as being used for epilepsy, the EEG is used to find out about brain function in a number of other illnesses.

Imaging

When a diagnosis of epilepsy is made, the treating doctor also tries to find out what has caused the epilepsy. If damage to the brain or a scar in the brain tissue is the likely cause then **imaging** will be used to try to find out the exact cause. There are many possible causes of symptomatic epilepsy ranging from birth injuries to **congenital malformations** of the blood vessels or structure of the brain.

CT and MRI are the two main imaging tests currently used. CT, which stands for Computed Axial Tomography, uses a combination of X-rays and computer technology to provide pictures through sections of the brain. CT is very useful for looking at bone structure, possible underlying causes such as a tumour and for emergencies such as when someone with a head injury has an epileptic fit. It is less useful in the investigation of focal epilepsy as certain subtle changes in brain structure may be missed. Any technique involving X-rays is always used with caution because of the harmful effects of too many X-rays during a lifetime, particularly for children.

MRI (Magnetic Resonance Imaging) uses a large and powerful magnet, microwave radiation and computers to generate detailed images of the inside of the body. The technique does not use X-rays and therefore does not carry any radiation risks. During an MRI scan the person will be asked to lie on a couch which is then moved into a narrow tunnel while the pictures are taken. It is necessary to lie still during the scan, which lasts for 20-40 minutes.
The machine makes a loud knocking noise while the pictures are being taken. Some people find lying still in the narrow tube rather claustrophobic and the noise of the machine quite unpleasant. Young children or adults who

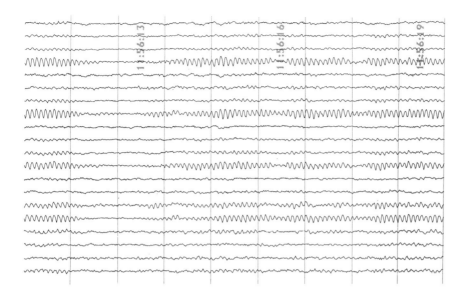

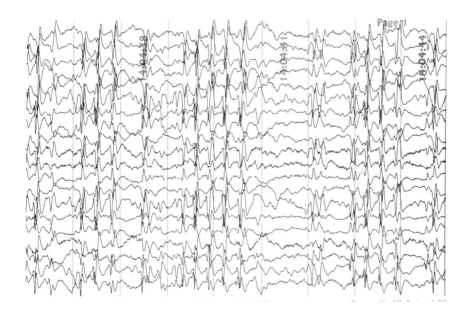

Figure 3: The top picture shows a normal EEG recording from a 30 year old man; the bottom picture is an EEG recording from an 11 year old boy taken during a generalised seizure.

experience these difficulties can be offered sedation (calming drugs) to help them undergo the test.

Imaging tests are not necessary for every patient with epilepsy. People with primary generalised seizures have normal scans and do not need imaging tests. Some people with partial seizures may need imaging depending on the age the epilepsy started, the type of fit and how well the epilepsy is controlled.

Other tests

Blood tests may sometimes be carried out for people who have been newly diagnosed with epilepsy or for people with chronic partially controlled seizures. These tests may provide information about the possible general causes of the epilepsy and also about the effects of long-term treatment with anti epileptic drugs.

An ECG (electrocardiogram) is occasionally carried out to check if heart problems may be responsible for some of the person's symptoms. The diagnosis of epilepsy is always made with great care as it can have effects on many aspects of the person's life. The effects can include long-term treatment with drugs, change in lifestyle, some changes to work practices, as well as the emotional effect of having a diagnosis of epilepsy. It sometimes takes several weeks before a definite diagnosis is made and anti-epileptic drugs are started. Most GPs do not make a definite diagnosis unless they are sure about the history of the problem and even then, most people will be referred to a specialist for confirmation of the diagnosis.

What drugs are used to treat epilepsy?

We have had anti-epileptic drugs (AEDs) for over 100 years. The effectiveness of AEDs in totally controlling various types of fit is dependent on many factors such as the person's age, gender, type of epilepsy and whether the person has any other medical conditions. The number of AEDs has increased dramatically over the past 10 years and new drugs have been added to more established ones. The choice of drug is at times difficult and has to be tailored to each person's particular needs.

AEDs are broadly divided into first and second line drugs. This is not due to their relative effectiveness but is historical and relates to the time they were introduced for general use. The first line drugs include phenobarbitone, phenytoin, primidone, carbamazepine, and sodium valproate. These drugs were introduced between the turn of the century and the middle sixties so they have been used for many years and their usefulness and side effects are well known.

Second line drugs are newer ones, which were introduced from the late eighties and have gone through thorough trial programmes before being licensed for use as AEDs. First line drugs were not tested in the way second line drugs were but they have stood the test of time. The second line drugs include (in the order in which they became available); vigabatrin, lamotrigine, gabapentin, topiramate and tiagabine. There are other, less widely used AEDs that are only used in epilepsy that is severe and resistant to treatment, such as clonazepam, clobazam, acetazolamide and ethosuxamide.

Sodium valproate

This is a first line AED that is mainly used to treat primary generalised epilepsy. It is effective and broad spectrum and therefore can also be used to treat partial seizures with and without generalisation. The drug, in the form of tablets or syrup is easy to take and depending on the particular brand, it is taken either once or twice a day. Unwanted reactions (side effects) can include stomach upset, weight gain, tremor, hair loss with re-growth of wavy hair, effects on the menstrual cycle and possible reduction in fertility and an increased risk of polycystic ovaries. There are some general side effects that occur to some extent with all AEDs and information on these is given on page 15.

Carbamazepine

This AED is used as the first line treatment for partial seizures with or without generalisation. It is not effective for primary generalised epilepsy and can actually increase some seizure types. The drug has to be started slowly and increased gradually over a few weeks to avoid some of the side effects, which can include rashes, drowsiness, balance problems, disturbed liver function and double vision. People taking carbamazepine will have regular blood tests to monitor the effect of the drug.

Phenytoin

Phenytoin is a standard AED that was introduced in the 1930s. It is effective for treating tonic clonic seizures but not for primary generalised epilepsy. It remains a very useful drug for some older patients and for those whose epilepsy is caused by a brain injury or tumour. However, it tends to be used less nowadays because of some of the side effects, which can include skin rashes, sedative effects, balance problems and double vision. When used over a long period of time, it can also cause acne, increased facial hair growth, coarsening of facial features, gum enlargement, disturbed liver function and interaction with other drugs which are processed by the liver. People taking phenytoin will have regular blood tests to monitor the effect of the drug.

Barbiturates (phenobarbitone and primidone)

Primidone appears to work by converting to phenobarbitone in the liver. These drugs are broad spectrum AEDs and have been used for most of this century. However, barbiturates have been used less over the past ten years, mainly because of the side effects. In children they can cause **hyperactivity syndrome** and in adults they can cause loss of concentration and effects on memory and drowsiness, which affects daily activities. Barbiturates are not used as initial drugs in the treatment of epilepsy; they are addictive drugs and because of this, there may be problems with drug withdrawal.

Vigabatrin

This drug, which was introduced in 1989, acts on a certain chemical messenger (neurotransmitter) in the brain called **GABA**. GABA is thought to suppress the electrical discharges of an epileptic fit and stop it spreading to other parts of the brain. As with all the newer drugs it was first tested in a group of patients whose epilepsy was not well controlled despite the use of multiple AEDs. Vigabatrin is given in twice daily doses and works in partial seizures with and without generalisation. This drug has been shown to be useful in one of the most severe forms of childhood epilepsy known as Lennox-Gastaut syndrome. However, side effects can include aggression, excitation, mental disorders and changes in vision.

Lamotrigine

This broad spectrum AED is used to treat both primary and partial seizure disorders. It needs to be started slowly and increased cautiously over several weeks to avoid skin rashes. The drug is given in twice daily doses and has been shown to be useful on its own (monotherapy) as well as in combination with other AEDs. It produces fewer effects on mental alertness compared to other AEDs. The drug can interact with others, particularly sodium valproate, and its use has to be carefully monitored.

Gabapentin

This AED is used in combination with other drugs for the treatment of epilepsy. The drug has to be used in three divided doses and it may be necessary to take six or more tablets a day. It does not interact with other drugs and can be started fairly quickly. Side effects are those seen in AEDs in general. Gabapentin is not used for the treatment of absence seizures.

Topiramate

Topiramate is another broad spectrum AED that is used to treat both primary and partial seizures. Twice daily dosing is used and it needs to be started slowly to avoid side effects. Drowsiness, confusion, impaired concentration, depression, aggression, kidney stones and loss of weight are possible side effects.

Tiagabine

This recently licensed AED works when added to other drugs in the treatment of partial secondary generalised epilepsy. It has similar side effects to other AEDs.

Other AEDs

There are other currently available drugs that are usually used as second or even third line drugs when major AEDs fail to control epilepsy. These are usually taken in combination with first line drugs and they include clobazam, clonazepam, diazepam, ethosuxamide and acetazolamide. There are also a number of other drugs which are currently being tested for the treatment of epilepsy but which are not yet licensed for use.

General side effects of AEDs

Most people with epilepsy will need to take AEDs for a number of years. Unwanted side effects of AEDs can include tiredness, nausea, poor memory and difficulty with concentration. However, drug side effects vary and can often be avoided with careful dosing and choice of the correct drug for each individual person. In high doses imbalance, double vision, and slurring of speech can occur. Your doctor will discuss possible side effects with you in detail.

It should be emphasised that AEDs are powerful drugs that act on the chemicals of the brain and should be taken according to the directions given to you by your doctor or specialist nurse. If the drugs are stopped suddenly there is a risk of more frequent fits and sometimes, continuous fitting (status epilepticus). As several drugs may be used together for the treatment of epilepsy, the effects of one drug on another (drug interaction) are important. Some anti-depressants and drugs used to treat some forms of mental illness may make the epilepsy worse and this has to be considered before they are used.

When should AEDs be started?

This very important question is not yet fully answered. Some people may have one or two fits in their lives without any apparent cause, while in others the seizure frequency can be much more, up to several times a day. When someone has a single seizure the decision to start AEDs is not straightforward. If there is no clear cause for the fit then AEDs may well be withheld until a second fit occurs. This practice, which is currently considered to be the most acceptable in the UK, is being studied by the Medical Research Council. Where a clear cause for a first fit can be found, then the likelihood of other fits occurring is high and AEDs are usually started straight away. The choice of the specific drug will depend on the type of epilepsy as well as the age and gender of the affected person and any other medication they may be taking.

Withdrawing AEDs

When the epilepsy is well controlled and there have been no seizures for more than three years, the possibility of withdrawing AEDs can be considered. There are certain types of epilepsy such as juvenile onset myoclonic epilepsy where it is not possible to safely withdraw AEDs. Where someone has generalised tonic clonic seizures after the age of 16 years, pre-existing brain damage or physical and learning disabilities, then withdrawal of AEDs is less likely to be successful.

Even if someone has been seizure free for years and has been driving cars, they will have to stop driving for the first six months of withdrawal from AEDs, and if they have a seizure then they will have to be free of fits for a further year before resuming driving. Generally speaking, up to a third of adults whose epilepsy is well controlled will experience fits again after slow withdrawal. Because of this it is important to take into account all the factors about the epilepsy before making a decision to withdraw AEDs.

General AED information

Anti-epileptic drugs should never be stopped suddenly as this could lead to recurrent fits or even status epilepticus, which is a very serious condition. Most AEDs are taken once or twice daily. After taking AEDs for a long time a certain level builds up in the body. Because of this there is no need to take a double dose if you forget a single dose. It is possible to drink alcohol while taking AEDs as long as it is occasional and in small amounts. Some people may find that the effects of alcohol are heightened by the AED medication.

Surgery and other treatment for epilepsy

Surgery may be helpful for a small number of people with epilepsy where a clear cause such as a tumour or vascular malformation (abnormality of the blood vessels) in the brain can be identified by CT or MRI scanning. Another group of people that may be helped by surgery are those with a scar in the brain tissue, usually in the temporal lobe of the brain. However this involves major brain surgery and is not undertaken lightly. The following criteria will usually need to be met before someone can be considered for epilepsy surgery:

1. There are no other major medical problems.

2. Anti-epileptic drug treatment is unsuitable or has been unsuccessful.

3. Seizures originate from a specific, identifiable area of the brain, usually the temporal lobe, which can be easily reached by surgery.

4. Normal brain function would not be damaged by operating on that part of the brain.

5. The person has a history of epilepsy, usually that started at an early age, or febrile convulsions as a child, frequent daytime complex partial seizures with minimal generalised activity and usually that they are under 40.

Investigation for epilepsy surgery
Several tests are usually carried out before surgery can be considered and the whole range of tests may take up to two years to complete. The tests include EEG, MRI scan, psychological and memory assessments and sometimes EEG video monitoring. Sometimes a **PET scan or subdural strip monitoring** is also necessary.

The surgery involves removing the part of the brain containing the damaged or abnormal structure. Modern imaging equipment, together with specialised surgical techniques mean that it is possible to very accurately locate the area to be removed and to reduce the risk of affecting healthy brain tissue.

The results of surgery in people who are selected according to these criteria are good, with control of the epilepsy being achieved in about two thirds of those who undergo the operation.

Following the surgery, there will usually be a stay in hospital of seven to 10 days, with a two to three month recovery period before it is possible to return to school or work. There is a small possibility (4-5% chance) of minor complications such as pain or infection around the operation site, but these can normally be effectively treated. More serious complications are very rare but include a 1-2% risk of stroke, memory impairment or visual disturbance.

AEDs are continued for at least a year after the operation before withdrawal can be considered. About one third of people who have undergone epilepsy surgery will need to remain on medication. Psychological and memory assessments, and MRI scans will be repeated after six months. People who have had successful epilepsy surgery often find they have to go through a period of adjustment to learn to live life without epilepsy. Follow-up care is usually continued for up to five years after the surgery.

A few specialised centres offer **non-invasive** surgical techniques such as radiosurgery, which uses a high-energy dose of radiation that can be focused on a precise point in the brain. These techniques and their long-term effects are still under investigation for the treatment of epilepsy.

Other methods of treatment include the use of nerve stimulation to stimulate the vagus nerve. This is useful for treatment of severe epilepsy where AEDs fail to control the seizures and where surgery is not considered to be feasible. During the treatment, a small electrical current generator is placed under the skin in the front part of the chest and wires stimulate the vagus nerve in the upper part of the neck.

First aid for a person who has had a fit

The first time you come across someone having a fit can be difficult or frightening, especially if the person is a family member or friend. Many people witnessing a fit for the first time dial 999 for an ambulance. By the time the paramedics arrive the fit will usually be over and the person will be recovering, although they may be a bit confused. It is not necessary to call an ambulance *unless* the fit lasts longer than five minutes, there are repeated fits or if the person has been injured during the fit.

Steve Gorton/Dorling Kindersley

Figure 4: A person placed in the correct recovery position to protect their airway and breathing

If you are present when someone has a fit, move any dangerous objects away from them and place a soft object such as a cushion or rolled-up jumper under their head. If possible, once the shaking has stopped, protect the head and turn the person's head and body to one side. This turning helps to protect their breathing. Trained first aiders should use the recovery position.

Do not try to put your finger or anything else in their mouth or remove any false teeth and do not try to hold onto the arms or legs to prevent jerking as this may actually cause damage to the limbs or to yourself. Just wait until the fit stops. It is possible that the person may cry out and sometimes their face may take on a bluish tinge due to a lack of oxygen. This will be followed by deep breathing and the appearance of froth at the mouth, which is sometimes tinged with blood if the tongue has been bitten. Sometimes there is loss of bladder control, or rarely, bowel control, during generalised tonic clonic seizures.

If the fit has not stopped after five minutes, call an ambulance. You will also need to call an ambulance if one fit follows another without the person regaining consciousness. This is known as status epilepticus and is a serious condition that requires urgent medical attention and treatment with **intravenous** AEDs. If you have epilepsy, it is important that someone close to you knows what to do.

How will life be affected?

The extent to which someone's life is affected depends on many factors including the cause of the epilepsy, the type of epilepsy, how well the epilepsy is controlled by AEDs, the nature of the person that is affected and the support available to them from friends, family and their workplace. The following sections provide information on some areas of lifestyle that are likely to be affected by a diagnosis of epilepsy.

Driving
Having epilepsy *does* affect the right to hold a UK driving license and you *must* inform the Driving and Vehicle Licensing Authority (DVLA) if you have been diagnosed with epilepsy. It is the DVLA, not your doctor that decides on an individual's eligibility to hold a driving license. The DVLA can obtain medical details from the doctors who are treating you (with your consent). People with epilepsy are barred from driving unless the following conditions are met:

Group 1 license
To hold a Group 1 license, which is for private cars and motorcycles, you must:

1. Have had one year of freedom from any epileptic fits up to the time when the license is granted OR

2. For people that have fits only during sleep, there has to have been a sleep-only pattern for three or more years, without fits whilst awake.

3. It must be confirmed that driving a car or motorcycle would not be a source of danger to the public. The DVLA will decide this based on your GP or consultant's recommendation.

The regulations about driving apply *whatever the type of epilepsy*. Even minor attacks will be counted. The requirement for a year of freedom from seizures applies whether or not a person is taking AEDs.

The regulations also deal with any unexplained loss of consciousness where no cause has been found. In this situation, the one year ban from driving also applies. One year after the last fit, you can obtain a three year license. A license that is valid to the age of 70 may be restored if you have been both free of fits and AEDs for ten years. Insurance companies may increase premiums for people with a past history of epilepsy.

Epileptic fits linked to misuse of alcohol or misuse of drugs whether prescribed or illicit also carry a one year ban and a medical review is required before the license can be reinstated. This is because some drugs, particularly those used to treat certain mental illnesses, have side effects that can affect a person's ability to drive safely.

Group 2 licence

To hold a Group 2 license, which is for heavy goods vehicles (HGVs) and passenger carrying vehicles that are more than 7.5 tonnes or carrying more than nine individuals you must:

1. Have been free from epileptic fits of any sort for the past 10 years and have had no anti-epileptic drugs during this 10 year period.

2. There is no likelihood of epileptic fits occurring. This mainly applies to people who have conditions that may cause epilepsy, such as severe head injury or complicated brain surgery.

If a specific cause for a one-off fit is known and there is no likelihood of further fits occurring, then these driving restrictions do not apply. Your doctor will provide advice but it is *up to individuals to inform the DVLA and not the doctor*. The responsibility for obeying the law rests with the individual, not the doctor. Your doctor's advice about driving will be recorded in your medical notes.

Women with epilepsy

Some women find that their fits are more likely to occur around the time of their menstrual period. Others find that this happens during the time just before their periods start, or around the time of ovulation. If this is the case then additional advice can be provided by your doctor or specialist nurse. Changing or adding other medication may help.

During the menopause some women find hormone replacement therapy (HRT) helpful and the effects are the same as for women without epilepsy. For women who have developed osteoporosis partly as a result of taking AEDs such as phenobarbitone and phenytoin, HRT may help. However, some AEDs affect the liver and cause the HRT to be processed more quickly so that higher doses of oestrogen hormone are required. Combination HRT may be more effective for some women with epilepsy. HRT itself does not seem to affect either epilepsy or the use of AEDs.

Becoming pregnant

Up to one in six couples in general may experience some difficulty in conceiving. Some of the rarer types of epilepsy and some AEDs may be linked to difficulties in conceiving. However *having epilepsy is not a bar to having children*. It is a good idea to have a discussion with your doctor before getting pregnant so that issues such as the dose of AEDs, monitoring the pregnancy, breast feeding and looking after the baby can all be considered.

Effects of AEDs on the baby

Usually women are advised not to take any drug during the first 12 weeks of pregnancy. However, having epilepsy makes an exception to that rule. This is because if AEDs are withdrawn altogether, there is a possibility of fits or even status epilepticus occurring, which could put both mother and baby at risk. To reduce the risks of any possible harm caused to the baby by AEDs, a single drug is usually used during pregnancy at the lowest possible dose, although the dose may need to be slightly increased in the later stages of pregnancy to take account of the increase in body size. The dose can usually be decreased again a month or so after birth. Folic acid supplements are also recommended for women who are trying to become pregnant.

Established AEDs (phenobarbitone, phenytoin, sodium valproate and carbamazepine) do increase the risk of birth defects. The risk has been estimated at 7-8% when a single drug is used. Potential problems with the pregnancy can usually be detected early during monitoring and can be discussed with the obstetrician or other doctor in charge of the care.

Labour

Having epilepsy does not interfere with normal labour and delivery. Women with epilepsy are usually advised to have their labour in hospital where the midwives and doctors are aware of the situation. AED use is continued throughout labour and additional drugs are not usually needed if the epilepsy is under control. Pain relief during labour is the same as for other mothers, however the use of pethidine is generally avoided. There may be a small increased risk of fits occurring in the first few days after giving birth.

Breast feeding

Mothers with epilepsy can breast feed their babies. A very small amount of any AED is secreted in the milk but this has not been shown to be harmful to the baby. For very young babies, breast feeding has to take place during the day and the night. As going without sleep can trigger fits, if the epilepsy control is incomplete, it may be a good idea for your partner or other family member to give some of the baby's feeds by bottle to allow you to catch some sleep.

Caring for your baby

Most women with epilepsy have normal pregnancies, births and cope well with their babies. If the epilepsy control is incomplete then some precautions are sensible. Feeding the baby while sitting on the floor with cushions around is a good idea to avoid dropping the baby if a fit does occur. Another good idea is to have someone around when you are bathing the baby.

Preventing pregnancy – oral contraception

Women with epilepsy can safely use the pill for contraception. Because some AEDs cause the liver to speed up the processing of various substances including the pill, it may be necessary to use the standard, rather than the mini dose pill. However if pregnancy is to be completely avoided the additional use of a barrier method such as the cap is usually recommended. A coil (intrauterine device) is another possibility, but there is a small risk of triggering a fit during insertion of the coil.

Daily activities at home

As with any one else, a person with epilepsy is responsible for his or her own safety. The amount of precautions you need to take depends on the severity of the epilepsy. It is a good idea to explain the situation to neighbours if you live on your own or to flatmates if you are sharing accommodation. It is also a good idea to let your family and friends know what to do if you have a fit (see page 19). People with epilepsy should be allowed and supported to lead as full and active a life as possible.

Cooking

If possible, try to avoid gas fires, but even electric cookers can burn. Useful tips are to turn the handles of saucepan away from the edge and try to avoid carrying containers of hot liquid by bringing plates and mugs to the cooker and kettle rather than carrying hot fluid across the kitchen.

Bathing

Showers are preferable to baths. It is a good idea to have a shallow bath if there is no shower. Let someone in the house know that you are having a bath especially if your epilepsy is partially controlled. If possible, avoid locking the bathroom door and if it is practical, have a door fitted that opens outward so that if you do have a fit, you don't prevent the door from being opened.

Stairs

When seizures are partially controlled, stairs can be dangerous. If at all possible it is a good idea to use the stairs as little as possible. For some people it may be necessary to move to a single storey home.

Work

Having epilepsy does not prevent anyone from working. However, some jobs such as those involving flying, deep sea diving, train driving and employment in the services are prohibited. People with active epilepsy are generally advised not to work at heights or with revolving machinery. Some employers may hesitate to employ a person with epilepsy simply because they do not have a full understanding of the condition and often wrongly believe that it will affect the person's ability to do their job.

Employers' insurance companies may sometimes impose specific clauses in insurance contracts that will need to be discussed with the occupational health officer. Every person will need to look at a prospective job and assess whether the epilepsy may lead to some difficulties for themselves or for work colleagues. You might wish to consider informing close work colleagues of the possibility of epilepsy to avoid alarm if a fit occurs out of the blue and so that they know how to give the correct first aid if necessary.

For people who develop epilepsy later in life, losing a job, for instance because of loss of their driving license, can be hard to accept. However, doctors do have a responsibility to protect their patients and society in general where a condition such as epilepsy is known to affect the ability to drive safely.

Leisure

Almost all leisure, social and sporting activities are open to people with epilepsy. Some activities however do carry an increased risk for people with epilepsy and should therefore be avoided. Examples include deep sea diving, para-gliding, deep caving, sky diving and mountaineering. Swimming is fine provided that you are accompanied by someone who knows about the possibility of a fit occurring and you have informed the lifeguards in public swimming pools. Youngsters can go on camping and cycling trips and other outdoor activities as long as their instructors are aware of their condition.

As far as possible, it is a good idea to avoid too much exposure to potential trigger factors such as alcohol, sleep shortage and stress. People with **photosensitive** epilepsy should consider limiting the time they spend watching TV or computer monitors. Sometimes, changing the frequency setting of the equipment or using blue tinted filters over the screen can reduce the likelihood of fits being triggered.

Relationships

Some people with epilepsy find that it can be difficult to accept being slightly different and having to take certain precautions regarding driving and regular intake of AEDs. Having epilepsy need not limit friendships or sexual relations. As far as possible, it is a good idea not to let epilepsy rule your life. When someone with epilepsy has difficulties, it may be their career who needs support to help them with their long-term caring role.

Support

Many people, when they are first diagnosed as having epilepsy, will turn to family and friends to discuss the diagnosis and the effect it may have on their life. After what may be an initial shock, there is often a period of adjustment to the new situation and the need to change some parts of their lifestyle. To some extent, this happens to everyone with epilepsy, but the effects and extent vary depending on the age of person with epilepsy.

If the person with epilepsy is a school-age child, their teachers will need to be informed so that they can manage the situation and monitor the effects of the condition on schoolwork. Sometimes special arrangements will need to be made to reduce the risk of fits occurring in times of increased stress, such as during exams.

Parents often face major decisions about their affected children and important decisions about plans for the family will have to be made. Doctors can help to some extent, but the time needed to discuss issues in detail may be lacking in the usual consultation in a GP's surgery or hospital visit.

There are a number of organisations with experience of the condition and its effects on people's lives and these are detailed on page 29 of this booklet. Social workers and community nurses can be very helpful. Epilepsy Nurse Specialists, who are hospital or community based, are available in many parts of the UK. They are experienced in offering advice and information to people with epilepsy and their families. Your local neurological centre may have contact details for epilepsy nurses in your area.

Glossary

Broad spectrum This term is used for drugs that have a range of activity against a variety of conditions, for example, broad spectrum antibiotics are active against a wide variety of bacterial infections.

Congenital malformation An abnormality that is present at birth, sometimes known as a birth defect. Congenital malformations can be inherited, or can occur as a result of damage or infection in the womb or during birth.

EEG This stands for electroecephalography, which is a test used to record the minute electrical impulses produced by the activity of the brain.

Encephalitis Inflammation of the brain, usually caused by a viral infection.

GABA This stands for gamma-aminobutyric acid. GABA is a neurotransmitter (a chemical that conveys messages within the nervous system) which controls the flow of nerve impulses by blocking the activity of other neurotransmitters.

Genetic This refers to the inherited instructions contained in the genes, which determine the activities of cells and therefore the development and functioning of the whole body.

Hyperactivity syndrome A condition in which children have difficulty concentrating and are constantly overactive.

Imaging Imaging techniques produce pictures of structures within the body that cannot otherwise be seen. Imaging techniques are very useful for diagnosing abnormalities and certain diseases.

Intravenous The introduction of a substance, usually fluid or drugs, directly into a vein.

Meningitis An infection of the coverings of the brain (the meninges).

Non-invasive A procedure that does not involve making an incision or introducing an instrument into the body for diagnosis or treatment.

PET scan Positron Emission Tomography scan. This is a scan that provides three-dimensional pictures that can show the chemical activity of the tissues being examined.

Photosensitive epilepsy Epilepsy that is triggered by exposure to flickering lights, such as disco strobe lights, or faulty fluorescent tube lighting. Only about five per cent of people with epilepsy are photosensitive.

Sensory perception The ability to see, hear, taste, smell and feel temperature, pressure and pain.

Strobe light A flashing beam of very bright light.

Subdural strip monitoring This procedure is only carried out in special cases and involves applying EEG electrodes to the surface of the brain after drilling four small holes in the skull while the person is under general anaesthetic.

Other organisations that may be able to help

Brain & Spine Helpline
British Brain and Spine Foundation
7 Winchester House
Kennington Park
Cranmer Road
London SW9 6EJ
Tel: 0808 808 1000
(Information and support on neurological disorders for patients, carers and health professionals)

Brain and Spinal Injury Charity (BASIC)
Neurocare Centre
554 Eccles New Road
Salford
Greater Manchester M5 2AL
Tel: 0870 750 0000
(Information, research and support groups)

British Epilepsy Association
Gate Way Drive
Yeadon
Leeds LS19 7XY
Tel: 0808 800 5050
(Information and advice)

DVLA Drivers' Medical Group
DVLA
Longview Road
Swansea, SA99 1DL
Tel: 0870 600 0301
Website: www.dvla.gov.uk

Epilepsy Association of Scotland
48 Govan Road
Glasgow G51 1LJ
Tel: 0141 427 4911
(Information and advice helpline)

Health Information Service
Tel: 0800 665544

(General health information and advice)

National Foetal Anti-convulsant Syndrome Association

Newton of Brux

Glenkindie

Aberdeenshire AB33 8RX

Tel: 019755 71340

(Information and support for parents whose children have been affected by anti-convulsant treatment)

National Society for Epilepsy

Chalfont St Peter

Gerrards Cross

Buckinghamshire SL9 ORJ

Tel: 01494 601400

(Medical support, counselling and information)

NHS Direct
Tel: 0845 4647

(Medical advice and information on NHS Services)

Supporting the work of the British Brain and Spine Foundation

In order for the British Brain and Spine Foundation to continue to fund its vital research and education work in brain and spine disorders, *we need your help.*

YES! I would like to help.
Please find enclosed a gift of £10 ☐ £15 ☐ £25 ☐ £ ☐ other

Name Mr/Mrs/Ms

Address

Postcode

or you may donate by Visa/Mastercard/CAF card by filling in the details below or calling us on 020 7793 5900

Card Number

☐☐☐☐ ☐☐☐☐ ☐☐☐☐ ☐☐☐☐

Expiry Date

☐☐ ☐☐

Signature

I am also interested in:
☐ *Making a Bequest*
☐ *Gift Aid*
☐ *Deed of Covenant*
☐ *Standing Order*
☐ *'Pennies to Pounds' – Fundraising for the BBSF*
☐ *Current Research and Education projects*
☐ *Volunteering*

British Brain and Spine Foundation, 7 Winchester House, Kennington Park, Cranmer Road, London SW9 6EJ Telephone: 020 7793 5900
Fax: 020 7793 5939 Registered charity no.1010067

Publications from British Brain and Spine Foundation

We can supply one copy of each relevant publication free to patients and carers affected by neurological disorders. However, if you are able to pay for them, it will help us to cover our costs. Additional copies cost £4 each for booklets and £3 each for leaflets. (Price includes £1.00 post and packing). Please make your cheque payable to the British Brain and Spine Foundation.

Please complete your name and address below, tick the appropriate box/es, and post your order to us at:

British Brain and Spine Foundation, FREEPOST, London SW9 6BR.

Name (Mr/Mrs/Miss/Ms) _____

Address _____

_____

_____ Postcode _____

Please tick as appropriate:

Aids and the brain	MRI Scan (leaflet)
Angiogram (leaflet)	Multiple sclerosis
Back & neck pain	Paralysis – the loss of muscle power
Brain tumour	Parkinson's disease
CT Scan (leaflet)	Speech, language and communication difficulties
Dizziness & balance problems	Stroke
Epilepsy	Sub-arachnoid haemorrhage
Headache	
Head injury & concussion	Transient ischaemic attacks and mild strokes
Meningitis & Encephalitis	

British Brain and Spine Foundation, 7 Winchester House, Kennington Park, Cranmer Road, London SW9 6EJ
Telephone: 020 7793 5900   Fax: 020 7793 5939

BRAIN & SPINE HELPLINE
0808 808 1000
Email: info@bbsf.org.uk   Registered Charity No. 1010067